HAL•LEONARD
INSTRUMENTAL PLAY-ALONG

AUDIO ACCESS INCLUDED

PLAYBACK+
Speed • Pitch • Balance • Loop

TRUMPET

Gospel Hymns

T0065898

To access audio visit:
www.halleonard.com/mylibrary

Enter Code
5771-6806-9129-2026

ISBN 978-1-4950-7383-0

HAL•LEONARD®
7777 W. BLUEMOUND RD. P.O. BOX 13819 MILWAUKEE, WI 53213

In Australia Contact:
Hal Leonard Australia Pty. Ltd.
4 Lentara Court
Cheltenham, Victoria, 3192 Australia
Email: ausadmin@halleonard.com.au

Visit Hal Leonard Online at
www.halleonard.com

AMAZING GRACE

TRUMPET

Words by JOHN NEWTON
Traditional American Melody

BLESSED ASSURANCE

TRUMPET

Lyrics by FANNY J. CROSBY
Music by PHOEBE PALMER KNAPP

DOWN BY THE RIVERSIDE

TRUMPET

African American Spiritual

HE'S GOT THE WHOLE WORLD IN HIS HANDS

TRUMPET

Traditional Spiritual

HIS EYE IS ON THE SPARROW

TRUMPET

Words by CIVILLA D. MARTIN
Music by CHARLES H. GABRIEL

IN THE GARDEN

TRUMPET

Words and Music by
C. AUSTIN MILES

LEANING ON THE EVERLASTING ARMS

TRUMPET

Words by ELISHA A. HOFFMAN
Music by ANTHONY J. SHOWALTER

THE OLD RUGGED CROSS

TRUMPET

Words and Music by
REV. GEORGE BENNARD

PRECIOUS MEMORIES

TRUPMET

Words and Music by
J.B.F. WRIGHT

SHALL WE GATHER AT THE RIVER?

TRUMPET

Words and Music by
ROBERT LOWRY

SWEET BY AND BY

Words by SANFORD FILLMORE BENNETT
Music by JOSEPH P. WEBSTER

TRUMPET

THERE IS POWER IN THE BLOOD

TRUMPET

Words and Music by
LEWIS E. JONES

Quickly, with energy
Lap steel guitar

WAYFARING STRANGER

TRUMPET

Southern American Folk Hymn

WHEN WE ALL GET TO HEAVEN

TRUMPET

Words by ELIZA E. HEWITT
Music by EMILY D. WILSON

WHISPERING HOPE

TRUMPET

Words and Music by
ALICE HAWTHORNE